Rugby is said to have been invented when William Webb Ellis picked up a football and ran with it.

WILLIAM WEBB ELLIS
1805 - 1872

Before matches, the All Blacks team performs the haka.

Before the match, the referee
tosses a coin to see which
team kicks off.

Rugby matches start with a dropkick.

In rugby, the ball is carried in hand.

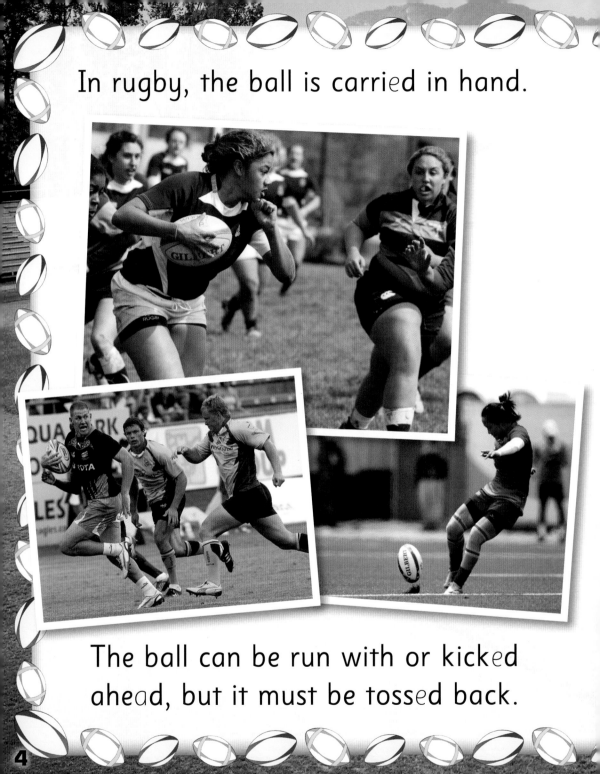

The ball can be run with or kicked ahead, but it must be tossed back.

To begin with, rugby balls were animal bladders with a leather outer shell.

Rugby is a contact sport. You have to tackle to get the ball.

In a scrum, everybody grips onto everybody else.

The ball is fed in and the hookers attempt to get it.

A rugby goal

crossbar

try line
/trie lien/

The aim is to score "tries."

Tries are when the ball is touched
on the ground across the try line.

To begin with, "tries" did not score points in rugby.

To "convert" tries into points, the ball had to be kicked across the crossbar.

In modern rugby, "tries" now score 5 points and you get 2 more points if you "convert."

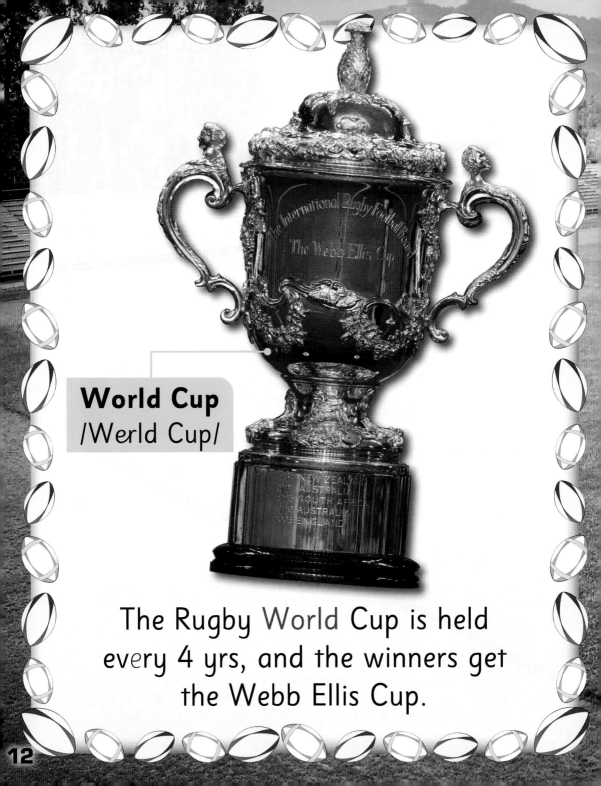

World Cup
/Werld Cup/

The Rugby World Cup is held
every 4 yrs, and the winners get
the Webb Ellis Cup.